LISTEI

Sketches and Monologues

by

MICHAEL FRAYN

SAMUEL FRENCH, INC.
45 WEST 25TH STREET   NEW YORK 10010
7623 SUNSET BOULEVARD HOLLYWOOD 90046
LONDON   TORONTO

IMPORTANT BILLING AND CREDIT REQUIREMENTS

CONTENTS

LISTEN TO THIS

HUSBAND. Good God. Good God. (*Looks over the top of his newspaper at his Wife.*) Good God.

WIFE. (*Lowers her newspaper.*) Sorry?

HUSBAND. A woman at a funeral in Essex yesterday was knocked down and killed by the hearse.

WIFE. (*Vaguely.*) Good God.

(*THEY both return to their newspapers.*)

HUSBAND. (*Without looking up.*) The Chancellor's been sounding off about various things.

WIFE. (*Without looking up.*) Good God.

HUSBAND. Fares are going up again.

WIFE. Good God.

HUSBAND. (*Surprised.*) Good God!

(*HE lowers his paper and waits until SHE has lowered hers.*)

WIFE. What?

HUSBAND. You remember that man we met at the Wrights' last week? The tall chap with glasses? Something to do with educational publishing?

WIFE. Yes.

HUSBAND. Remember where his wife came from?

WIFE. No?

HUSBAND. Prestonpans. Just outside Edinburgh. I remember thinking at the time what an odd name it was. Well, they had a freak storm there yesterday.

(*SHE waits. HE goes back to his paper.*)

WIFE. Is she all right?
HUSBAND. Is who all right?
WIFE. The wife of the man we met at the Wrights'?
HUSBAND. She doesn't live there *now*. Obviously. Since she lives *here*. But a number of trees were uprooted.

(*THEY read for a while.*)

HUSBAND. Good God! Do you know how much money people in this country spent on potato crisps last year?
WIFE. (*Without looking up.*) Six million pounds.
HUSBAND. Six million pounds! (*HE shakes his head and laughs, then looks up.*) What did you say?
WIFE. I didn't say anything.
HUSBAND. I thought you said something. You're always trying to tell me things when I'm reading.

(*THEY read.*)

HUSBAND. (*HE laughs.*) How about this? 'An Electricity Board official said last night that the Board's computer had apparently gone hoywire.'
WIFE. (*Vaguely.*) Good God.
HUSBAND. (*Stops laughing.*) Oh. I'm talking to myself, am I?
WIFE. No, I was listening. An official said the computer had gone haywire.

HUSBAND. Hoywire.

WIFE. That's obviously a misprint.

HUSBAND. Yes. (*HE returns to his paper.*)

WIFE. (*SHE looks at him.*) Listen to this, then. 'Officials in La Paz were last night expressing cautious optimism about Paraguay's apparently more flexible line on talks. They were commenting on reports that Paraguay had dropped its insistence on the exclusion of relations with Chile from the agenda as a precondition for any meeting.'

HUSBAND. What's funny about that?

WIFE. Nothing at all.

HUSBAND. Not very surprising, is it?

WIFE. Not at all surprising.

HUSBAND. We don't know anyone who lives in La Paz, do we?

WIFE. I don't think so. There aren't any misprints either. I thought it would make a change from the news in your paper.

HUSBAND. (*Goes back to his paper, hurt.*) And I thought marriage was supposed to be something to do with sharing.

CONFESSION

What else? Well, I've been guilty of the sin of anger. I've shouted at my children several times during the past week. As Thou hast, of course, seen, with Thy All-Seeing Eye. And no doubt heard, with Thy All-Hearing Ear.

And then again I've committed malice on a number of occasions. I was definitely trying to hurt my sister's feelings that time. I mean on Tuesday. When my sister—this is my younger sister, I'm talking about, Janice, the one who lives just outside Watford ... Well, of course, Thou knowest which sister I mean. I always forget that with Thy All-Knowing Mind Thou knowest perfectly well what I mean. Much better than *I* do, in fact. I only went to see her on Tuesday at all, I have to confess, because I was over in that direction anyway, visiting Mother in the nursing home, which as Thou knowest I always try to do at least once a week—I mean, not of course that I want to boast about it—it's the very least I can do—in fact I feel terrible about not having her at home, as Thou knowest ...

Or did I drop it into the conversation like that to make Thee think better of me? Well, Thou knowest whether I did or not, and if Thou thinkest I *did* then I repent it *at once*, as I try to do with *all* my unworthy thoughts and actions ...

Hold on—where was I, before I got sidetracked like that? (Another of my faults, incidentally, for which I'm extremely sorry.) I was in the middle of repenting something. ... Well, Thou knowest perfectly well what

I was going to say, so if I can't remember perhaps Thou couldst take it as repented all the same ...

Oh, no, I know, my sister. Yes, when she started to go on about Mother and Mrs. Wemyss (who, as Thou knowest, runs the nursing home) and I said, 'Janice, I honestly do not want to sit here and listen to you going on about that woman, who has been so *kind* to Mother,' and Janice turned to me and gave me one of those looks of hers ...

Well, of course, Thou sawest the whole incident. If I mention the words 'gooseberry jam' I'm sure Thou knowest exactly what I'm repenting of. And of course when I said how clever I thought her children's drawings were, Thou weren'test fooled for a moment. Nor was she, of course.

Anyway, I'm truly sorry. In fact I've been brooding about it ever since. And that's another thing I ought to mention—the way I think about myself all the time. I mean, whenever I'm not actually busy doing something wrong I'm thinking about how wrong it was. Dost Thou know what I mean? Well, of course Thou dost.

This seems to me to be my worst sin of all. I don't know whether Thou wouldst agree. Or wait a minute, though. Am I just thinking this as an excuse for *not* thinking perpetually about my sins? Anyway, *Thou* knowest for certain what I'm up to, and whatever it is I'm really and truly sorry about it. Aren't I?

AT THE SIGN OF THE RUPTURE BELT

NICOLETTE. There's the shop with the rupture belt outside! Now we've driven halfway to Granny's, haven't we, Daddy?

FATHER. Halfway exactly.

NICOLETTE. I always remember we're halfway when we get to the shop with the rupture belt outside, don't I, Daddy?

DOMINIC. And I always remember we're three-quarters way when we get to Acme Motors, don't I, Daddy?

MOTHER. I wish you two would stop your silly pestering. I don't know why we bring you out in the car to Granny's.

FATHER. It's good for them to travel, Eileen. They see new things. They get something fresh to talk about.

DOMINIC. There's the factory with the rusty bike on the roof!

NICOLETTE. There's the advertisement for Viriloids Rejuvenating Pills!

DOMINIC. There's the Tigers!

MOTHER. The *what?*

DOMINIC. The Tigers! That's what we always call the Lyons there, don't we, Daddy?

FATHER. We certainly do, son. And there's the brewery where they brew the Adam's ale.

NICOLETTE. Daddy always says that now when we pass the Wemblemore waterworks, doesn't he, Dominic? He never used to, did he?

FATHER. What's this place on the right, children?

DOMINIC. I know! I know! It's the site for the new eye hospital.

NICOLETTE. Say your joke, Daddy, say your joke!

FATHER. It's a proper site for sore eyes.

NICOLETTE. Did you hear Daddy say his joke, Mummy?

MOTHER. Are we in Sudstow yet, John?

DOMINIC. Mummy, you *never* know where this is. You always ask Daddy if we're in Sudstow when we get to the site for sore eyes.

FATHER. Where are we then, Mr. Knowall?

DOMINIC. We're just coming to the place where we saw the drunk men fighting—

NICOLETTE. —where Daddy always says: "Can you imagine a more godforsaken hole than this?"

DOMINIC. And Mummy says she can't.

FATHER. We're just coming into Surley, Eileen.

DOMINIC. And you're not sure, are you, Daddy, but you think Wemblemore ends and Surley begins just after Wile-U-Wate Footwear Repairs, don't you?

FATHER. Look at it, Eileen. Scruffy people, cheapjack stores, rundown cinemas. I wonder how many pubs there are in this street alone?

DOMINIC. There are nine, Daddy.

NICOLETTE. We always count them for you.

FATHER. Can you imagine a more godforsaken hole?

NICOLETTE. Daddy said it, Dominic.

DOMINIC. Now say you can't, Mummy.

MOTHER. Oh, do stop pestering. Can't you think of some game to play as we go along?

DOMINIC. We *are* playing a game, Mummy. But you're not playing it properly.

NICOLETTE. You haven't said you can't imagine such a god-forsaken hole, has she, Dominic?

MOTHER. Those children! They're enough to try the patience of a saint!

FATHER. There's Acme Motors, anyway—we're three-quarters of the way there now.

DOMINIC. *Daddy!* That's what *I* say! *I'm* the one who sees Acme Motors and says we're three-quarters of the way there!

NICOLETTE. Yes, Daddy, that's *Dominic's* thing to say!

FATHER. Well, I've said it now.

NICOLETTE. But that's not fair, Daddy! You say: "I hope to God there's not going to be a holdup in Sudstow High Street."

DOMINIC. You've *spoilt* it, Daddy, you've *spoilt* it! You've said my thing!

NICOLETTE. Now you've made Dominic cry.

FATHER. Calm down, Dominic. Be your age.

DOMINIC. How would you like it if I said your things? How would you like it if I said "A site for sore eyes"?

MOTHER. Don't be disrespectful to your father, Dominic.

DOMINIC. I don't care! *A site for sore eyes! A site for sore eyes! A site for sore eyes!*

MOTHER. If you don't stop this instant, Dominic, I'm going to ...

NICOLETTE. Daddy, Daddy! We've gone past Cook and Cook (Wholesale Tobacconists) and you haven't said your joke about spoiling the breath!

FATHER. Oh, dry up.

MOTHER. Now they're both howling. It's all your fault, John. They just copy you.

FATHER. That's what you always say.

MOTHER. And that's what *you* always say!

FATHER. Well, all I can say is, I hope to God there's not going to be a holdup in Sudstow High Street.

A LITTLE PEACE AND QUIET

A garden. Sunshine. Two chairs.

WIFE. He won't think of anything out here. I could tell him that. The lawn sprinkler going all the time. The birds singing. It's not the right atmosphere. Not for him. Why doesn't he go inside? Get a bit of peace and quiet. It's ridiculous. Every day. Sitting here. Sitting in the kitchen watching me give Mrs. Henty her instructions. No wonder he can't think of anything.

HUSBAND. He's talking to them again. Talking to the dogs. I've never heard of that, talking to guard dogs. They should be like wild animals. They shouldn't be talked to. What does he say to them?

WIFE. That play about the blind beggar. He didn't think of that sitting in a garden listening to the birds. It was in that basement flat we had. You'd lie in bed at night and you'd hear noises. Some old man coming down the area steps to relieve himself. Women taking men on to the bomb-site next door. And screams. A lot of screams. You never found out afterwards what it had been.

HUSBAND. You make a bit of money. You've a few pounds coming in. All you want is a little peace and quiet. You hire someone to keep an eye on things. Feed the dogs. Patrol the grounds. Keep out intruders. I said to him: "You seem quiet enough." He said: "Ay, quiet enough." And then you find him whispering to the dogs.

WIFE. One night in January. Huddling round the oil-heater. The window was broken—some kids trying to get in. He sat there very quiet. Just staring into the heater. I didn't say anything. I could see he'd got an idea. I always know. That was the play about the couple who take in this blind beggar. You never discover his name. Slowly he takes over the house. He puts on the husband's clothes. He moves into bed with the wife. While the husband goes slowly blind as well.

HUSBAND. I look out at night sometimes, after the house is locked up. I see him making his rounds in the dusk. Swinging his stick. Suddenly he'll hit out at a tree. Crack! I can't see what the expression is on his face.

WIFE. Yes, and that play where the man who came to read the meter stayed and took over the house, and raped the wife, and kept the husband as a servant—he didn't think that up sitting in a garden.

HUSBAND. And what happened last week, when the man called to read the meter? I'd given my man his instructions. I'd told him: "Any meter-readers, that kind of thing, you stay with them and watch them until they're off the premises. Make sure the meter's the only thing they touch." He stayed with him all right. They were in the stables looking at those meters for fifteen minutes or more. Talking together. What about?

WIFE. Nor the one about the two men who came to the house claiming to be old school friends of the husband's. That was the one where the husband couldn't remember them, so they decide to share the wife between the three of them as a compromise. He thought of that while his brother was living with us.

Thought   of it on the area steps. There wasn't anywhere else to think.

HUSBAND. He came to see me the other day. He said: "There's a man at the gate says he may have known your wife in Streatham." I said: "There's very little I want in life. I want peace and quiet. That's all. Just peace and quiet. This is why I employ you. This is the reason for your presence in the lodge. This is why I spend the money I've earned on your services." He said: "This man's ill. He's dying. In the road." I said: "There are some leaves in the pool need getting out." He looked at me then. Didn't say anything. Looked.

WIFE. He could write his plays then! Oh yes! People coming to the door all the time, but it didn't seem to put him off. The rent collector. Old men from the spike. People to repossess the furniture. Men in white mackintoshes who said they'd known him years before in Stevenage. They'd walk about the rooms, putting their hands on our things, looking at my breasts. Never a moment's peace and quiet.

HUSBAND. Look at the way he walks. Slowly. Thoughtfully. No expression on his face. Touching things as he passes. Getting to know them. Putting a value on them. He looks at her like that. When I'm not there. I know. Looks at her breasts. Thinking, one day …

(*Pause.*)

WIFE. He's thought of something. About time. Now maybe we'll get a little peace and quiet.

BLOTS

(*Thinks.*) *Relax, relax, relax. They certainly won't take you if you seem nervous. They don't want neurotics for a job like this. Sit quite still. Look completely impassive. Don't think. Mind a blank ... He spoke!*

(*Speaks.*) What?

Did he speak?

Sorry...? Giddiness? Do I suffer from giddiness? No?

What's he writing? It can't take him all that long to write "no." He's writing some comment on the way I said it.

What? Fits? No.

Don't sit there snapping "no" like that! Don't sound so defensive! He'll think there's something you're trying to hide. Be natural! Be conversational!

Blackouts? No, no, no. No blackouts. Never. Never. No, no, no.

That was dreadful. Did you see the way he looked at you? Be amused by it all! Sit back and enjoy it! Make jokes! Smile!

Psychiatric treatment? No, I've never had psychiatric treatment.

What's he driving at? Never mind—smile! Make conversation!

One of my aunts is rather eccentric. I mean, who can say exactly where the borderline is between eccentricity and madness? It must be established by the people around one, by the society in which one lives ...

Keep going!

The place my aunt lives in is Matlock. It's in Derbyshire. Do you know Derbyshire at all? I love the Peak District. I love the countryside. I'm interested in ... natural things. But no, I've never had psychiatric treatment.

Oh God! He thinks I'm crazy! Well, don't look crazy, then! Go on being amused!

Intrusive? These questions? Not at all! Anyway, I love intrusive questions! Intrude away!

No! No more laughs! Just smile! He thinks I'm insecure, doesn't he. He thinks I'm unstable. He'll start giving me mental tests next.

What? Look at what? What card? Where?

Ink blots! Oh my God, it's the ink blots! He's giving me the ink blots! I knew it!

What can I see? Well, that's a ... It's a sort of ... well ... it looks like a kind of ...

I mustn't see any blood! I mustn't see any phallic symbols, or violence, or threatening clouds, or ...

Two drunken men! It's two drunken men fighting, isn't it? No, no, no! I don't mean that!

No violence!

I mean two women kissing each other. No, sorry! I'm saying the first thing that comes into my head. But of course that's what you want me to do. Well, then, it's a man. It's a man standing with his legs apart—I mean a woman lying with her ... No, no, no, I mean it's a man with a, well, a large kind of thing ... No! No! No! Quick! What do I mean? I mean, it's a father hitting his child with an axe ... I don't mean that at all. I mean it's a woman who's been split down the middle ... This is absurd! These things are saying themselves!

Deep breath. Deep breath. Now, start all over again.

Yes. Now I've got it. It's a sort of *calm* kind of scene. I mean, there's no conflict in it. There's no sex. There's no blood, or anything like that. It's a kind of natural scene ... in the countryside ... with grass and trees ... and a thatched cottage ... and cows ... No! No cows! Oh, yes—cows ... and so on ...

Why's he looking at me like that? He thinks I'm trying to avoid conflict and sex. He thinks I'm repressing them.

I mean, there's a little sort of natural violence in the picture. The sort of violence you get in nature. I don't know—I think two of the cows are fighting. In a friendly way. And sex—there's some sex, too. Once again I see it as being somehow kind of natural. I think two of the cows ... I mean a cow and a bull ... Well, some of the birds ...

Oh dear. Oh dear.

Go? Go where ...? Oh. You mean you've finished? But don't you want to do any more tests ...? I suppose that means I've failed. Does it? You won't accept me for aircrew training? It's so unfair! I'm not neurotic normally! I'm only neurotic because I'm sitting here having questions fired at me! If I'd just been sitting here looking at that ink blot without people shouting at me and putting pressure on me I'd have thought it looked like something entirely different! Something more like a ... I don't know—where's the card...? Something more like ... A. It's a letter A! Hold on ... G M T X Q R B ...This is an eye-test! Well, how am I supposed to see it's an eye-test if I haven't got my glasses on?

THROUGH THE WILDERNESS

MOTHER. It is nice now that all you boys have got cars of your own. You know how much it means to me when the three of you drive down to see me like this, and we can all have a good old chatter together.

JOHN. That's right, Mother, So, as I was saying, Howard, I came down today through Wroxtead and Sudstow.

HOWARD. Really? I always come out through Dorris Hill and West Hatcham.

RALPH. I find I tend to turn off at the traffic lights in Manor Park Road myself and follow the 43 bus route through to the White Hart at Broylesden.

MOTHER. Ralph always was the adventurous one.

JOHN. Last time I tried forking right just past the police station in Broylesden High Street. I wasn't very impressed with it as a route, though.

HOWARD. Weren't you? That's interesting. I've occasionally tried cutting through the Broylesden Heath Estate. Then you can either go along Mottram Road South or Creese End Broadway. I think it's handy to have the choice.

RALPH. Of course, much the prettiest way for my money is to carry on into Hangmore and go down past the pickles factory in Sunnydeep Lane.

MOTHER. Your father and I once saw Lloyd George going down Sunnydeep Lane in a *wheelbarrow* ...

HOWARD. Did you, Mother? I'm not very keen on the Sunnydeep Lane way personally. I'm a great believer in turning up Hangmore Hill and going round by the pre-fabs on the Common.

RALPH. Yes, yes, there's something to be said for that, too. What was the traffic like in Sudstow, then, John?

JOHN. Getting a bit sticky.

HOWARD. Yes, it was getting a bit sticky in Broylesden. How was it in Dorris Hill, Ralph?

RALPH. Sticky, pretty sticky.

MOTHER. The traffic's terrible round here now. There was a most frightful accident yesterday just outside when ...

HOWARD. Oh, you're bound to get them in traffic like this. Bound to.

RALPH. Where did you strike the traffic in Sudstow, then, John?

JOHN. At the lights by the railway bridge. Do you know where I mean?

RALPH. Just by that dance hall where they had the trouble?

JOHN. No, no. Next to the neon sign advertising mattresses.

HOWARD. Oh, you mean by the caravan depot? Just past Acme Motors?

JOHN. Acme Motors? You're getting mixed up with Heaslam Road, Surley.

HOWARD. I'm pretty sure I'm not, you know.

JOHN. I think you are, you know.

HOWARD. I don't think I am, you know.

JOHN. Anyway, that's where I struck the traffic.

RALPH. I had a strange experience the other day.

JOHN. Oh, really?

RALPH. I turned left at the lights in Broylesden High Street and cut down round by the back of Coalpit Road. Thought I'd come out by the

Wemblemore Palais. But what do you think happened? I came out by a new parade of shops, and I thought, hello, this must be Old Hangmore. Then I passed an Odeon—

JOHN. An Odeon? In Old Hangmore?

RALPH. —and I thought, that's strange, there's no Odeon in Old Hangmore. Do you know where I was? In *New* Hangmore!

HOWARD. Getting lost in New Hangmore's nothing. I got lost last week in Upsome!

JOHN. I went off somewhere into the blue only yesterday not a hundred yards from Sunnydeep Lane!

MOTHER. I remember I once got lost in the most curious circumstances in Singapore ...

RALPH. Anybody could get lost in Singapore, Mother.

JOHN. To become personal for a moment, Howard, how's your car?

HOWARD. Not so bad, thanks, not so bad, And yours?

JOHN. Not so bad, you know, How's yours, Ralph?

RALPH. Oh, not so bad, not so bad at all.

MOTHER. I had another of my turns last week.

HOWARD. We're talking about cars, Mother. *Cars.*

MOTHER. Oh, I'm sorry.

JOHN. To change the subject a bit—you know where Linden Green Lane comes out, just by Upsome Quadrant?

HOWARD. Where Turnstall Road joins the Crescent there?

RALPH. Just by the Nervous Diseases Hospital?

JOHN. That's right. Where the new roundabout's being built.

HOWARD. Almost opposite a truss shop with a giant model of a rupture belt outside?

RALPH. Just before you get to the bus station?

HOWARD. By the zebra crossing there?

JOHN. That's right. Well, I had a puncture there on Friday.

RALPH. Well, then, I suppose we ought to think about getting back.

HOWARD. I thought I might turn off by the paint factory on the by-pass this time and give the Apex roundabout a miss.

JOHN. Have either of you tried taking that side road at Tillotson's Corner?

RALPH. There's a lot to be said for both ways. A lot to be said.

MOTHER. I'll go and make the tea while you discuss it, then. I know you've got more important things to do than sit here listening to an old woman like me chattering away all afternoon.

NEVER MIND THE WEATHER

We've just been on our first cruise! Yes, our first one ever! Oh, we had a lovely time! We're quite converted! Beautiful boat, it was. Oh, an absolutely first-class boat. Not one of those big luxury liners where you have to change for dinner. We shouldn't fancy that. That's not our style. No, nice little boat. Well, about 300 cubits long. Made of gopher wood, which I believe is very good for making boats out of. And a nice homey atmosphere. In fact it was more for cargo than passengers, really. Cattle, and pigs, and sheep, and that type of thing. Oh, we're all very fond of animals so it didn't worry us! The weather was a bit, you know, *mixed*. But it didn't matter, you felt you were seeing the world. Don't ask me where we went exactly—we went all over the place! All round the Holy Land, all round there. And we finished up by putting in at that famous mountain they've got out there. What's it called? Not Vesuvius. It'll come to me in a minute. We were rather pleased to see it, actually! We'd had one or two days quite bad weather, you see. Oh yes, it was quite bad at times. But it didn't worry us.

That's the wonderful thing about a cruise. You don't have to go out. You've got all the entertainment provided. So we didn't care if it rained all the time. Well, you make your own fun, don't you? The whole family was there, after all. Oh, yes! We all went! My husband and I—his brother Shem and his wife—Ham and his wife. And the boys brought their Mum and

Dad! Sweet! You should have seen us all! You'd have thought we owned the ship! In fact, we were the only passengers. So we had the run of it. Which was nice. Talk about fun and games! Particularly when the weather was bad! Oh, they all said the same thing, they all said they'd never seen anything like it before. Half the time we really and truly didn't know whether we were ever going to see land again. I said to Dad, I said, "At least the rats haven't deserted us!" Because we had rats on board. Not many. You'd see one or two from time to time. Yes, the storm lasted forty days, non-stop! They sent off a pigeon at one point, to see if it could get a message through. It was as bad as that. Still, it was a holiday, that's the main thing. And I took a lovely picture of the rainbow—I've got it here somewhere. Well it's lovely of Japhet—the rainbow didn't come out.

VALUE FOR MONEY

Oh, you live in the North, do you? How super.
What fun. You don't by any chance know the
Uzzards? They live in the North somewhere. He's in
some terrific chemical thing up there, and she's
hideously pretty. I mean, I hardly know them, but I do
remember someone saying they lived up in that part
of the world. You *must* meet them, they're *frightful*
sweeties. Well, I say they're up in the North, but of
course at the moment they aren't because he's doing
... what is he doing? How is it that one can never
remember what people are doing? I think he's doing
five years. I *think* I'm right in saying five. There was
some terrible confusion about some money thing he
was mixed up with. Such a pity, because he's such
good value. And she's so madly sensible about it all.
And the absolutely unforgivably ghastly thing is that
I've forgotten what *she's* doing, but I think what she's
doing is life. There was some kind of dreadful muddle
about her au pair getting sort of murdered. *Such*
rotten luck. And of course just when she needed the
girl most! Maddening when you get a good one, and
off she goes. Because the tragic thing was, the girl
was an absolute marvel. I think that's why David got
involved in this terrible confusion about the money
thing. I *think* so. There was some ghastly mix-up over
sort of fur coats and abortion sort of things . I *think* that
was it. Then Sue heard that David had got involved in
this muddle about the money thing and she thought,
wow, and *she* got into this muddle about the murder

thing. So absolutely awful when everyone involved is so awfully nice. And such killingly good value. But you've never met them? And now they're not up in the North any more! How sickening. Such a dreadful waste, somehow. No, I mean of the North. Still, I get the impression it's frightful fun living up there.

THE PROPERTY SPECULATORS

MOTHER. What a lucky old woman I am! Having three sons so good to me! You know how much I appreciate your finding the time to take me for a run in the motor like this.

JOHN. You just sit back and enjoy the view, Mother. What do you reckon that one is, then, Ralph?

RALPH. The one with the crazy-paving washdown? Oh, two hundred, John, at least.

JOHN. *Two hundred?* Two hundred and fifty, more likely.

HOWARD. What about that one there, with all the wrought iron on the sun lounge?

RALPH. Must be getting on for two - fifty, Howard.

JOHN. Nearer three hundred, I'd say. I mean, you know where we are—the Wroxtead Valley estate.

HOWARD. Oh, it's pricey round here all right. I'm not denying. it.

RALPH. Especially up this end. Aren't we just coming out at that five-way junction on the Surley by-pass?

JOHN. That's right. By that new roadhouse there, the Olde Shippe.

RALPH. Hey, look at that one then! With the Jag outside!

JOHN. I'll tell you what, Ralph. I bet that's three-fifty.

MOTHER. Three-fifty what, dear?

HOWARD. The *house,* Mother. The house is three-fifty.

JOHN. Here's the by-pass, then. Now where?

RALPH. How about cutting down Hatcham Park Road to North Sudstow? We could try out the new underpass in Sudstow Village on the way back.

JOHN. Fair enough.

MOTHER. Talking about houses reminds me of a house your grandfather's brother Tom once owned. It was somewhere overlooking the river in Chelsea, and Whistler was supposed to have ...

JOHN. Yes, but who wants to live in the middle of London, Mother? Pricey round here, you know, Ralph, in Hatcham Park.

RALPH. Pretty pricey.

JOHN. I don't know what one of these houses would cost you.

HOWARD. Oh, a packet, John a real packet.

RALPH. I mean, I know a chap in the office—nice chap, got a couple of kids, one of them suffers rather badly from asthma—and his brother-in-law bought, not one of these houses, but one of those big ones up by the cemetery at Upsome. You know where I mean? Well, that cost him close on two hundred, and it wasn't anything like one of these. And that was five years ago, when prices just weren't comparable.

JOHN. I know. I know.

RALPH. What one of these would cost you I don't know.

MOTHER. Ralph always was the clever one.

HOWARD. This is more or less North Sudstow here.

JOHN. Not cheap here, you know.

HOWARD. Quite pricey, by the look of it. What would you say that one with the Spanish-type porch would cost?

JOHN. Must be three hundred at the very least, mustn't it?

RALPH. What about that new split-level ranch house, then, with the latticed dormer windows? Stop for a moment, John, and let's have a look at it.

MOTHER. Are we going for a walk?

JOHN. No, no, Mother. Just you sit back and admire the scenery. Shall I tell you what I think, Ralph? This may surprise you, Ralph, but it's really and truly what I think—

HOWARD. Go on.

JOHN. Three-fifty.

RALPH. Three-fifty? You may be right at that. I was going to say three, three-twenty-five.

JOHN. Fourteen. Ah well, let's press on.

MOTHER. Wouldn't it be nice if one day we could go out into the country on one of these runs? But then I suppose there's no country left these days.

JOHN. Country, Mother? This *is* the country. We're in the Green Belt here.

HOWARD. Can't you see the grass verges, Mother?

RALPH. Her eyesight's going, you know.

JOHN. Know this road we're joining now? The Vale, Sudstow. You could have got one of these houses here for a song 10 years ago. They couldn't give them away.

HOWARD. Fantastic, isn't it? Some of these people must have mopped up three or four hundred percent profit.

RALPH. Does something to you to think about it, doesn't it?

HOWARD. Beats me the way human beings carry on about things like houses. You'd think they'd have other things to think about.

JOHN. Now I've got a real surprise for you. It's a little road I discovered the other day by pure accident. This next one on the right—Bolderwood Avenue. Take a look at it. They don't make them much pricier than this.

HOWARD. Very pricey indeed, John.

RALPH. You certainly know how to pick them.

HOWARD. Look at that one with the weather-boarding on the gables! I should think the garages alone must have cost fifty thousand!

RALPH. It's marvellous what you can spend, isn't it, when you come down to it?

HOWARD. What do you think these places would fetch? Half a million?

RALPH. Three quarters.

HOWARD. Three quarters plus.

JOHN. It'd be wrong to guess, Howard. There are some things in life you can't reckon in figures alone.

HOWARD. You're right there.

RALPH. Ah, it's a real tonic just to look at them.

JOHN. Well then, home James?

MOTHER. It *is* good of you boys to bother with me, taking me out to see the world like this. It's a pleasure just to listen to you—my word, how you do appreciate everything you set your eyes on!

WHO DO YOU THINK YOU ARE?

WOMAN. (*Carrying a tray with a cup of tea on it.*) Excuse me, is this seat ...?

MAN. No, no.

(*SHE sits down and sips her tea.*)

MAN. Usually in here around this time, aren't you?

WOMAN. Come in about quarter to six, ten to six, usually.

MAN. Yes, I'm usually in here around this time. Have a cup of tea before I go home. Calm down.

WOMAN. I need my cup of tea today.

MAN. One of those days?

WOMAN. Terrible.

MAN. Should have seen mine. I say you should have seen *my* day!

WOMAN. Some people seem to think if you work in a shop you're just there to lick their boots.

MAN. Oh, that sort.

WOMAN. Treat you like dirt. Think they're the Lord High Executioner.

MAN. You should have my job.

WOMAN. "Haven't got it in stock?" "I'm sorry, Madam." "This is disgusting. I shall write to the Managing Director and complain." "Yes, Madam."

MAN. I say, you should have my job.

WOMAN. They just want someone to take it out on.

MAN. They ring me up. Why haven't the men turned up to repair the central heating? Half the time they've been, and there was no one there.

WOMAN. They really make me sick.

MAN. Get quite nasty, some of them. You know, sarcastic. It's the phone that does it. You're just a voice to them. They wouldn't dare say it to your face.

WOMAN. A man rang up today. Complained he'd had to wait half an hour to be served.

MAN. I had a woman on the phone this afternoon. Told me she was going to ring the Chairman at home to complain.

WOMAN. Then he waxed very sarcastic. Wanted to know if he'd get a prize to mark the occasion. Nothing to do with me—I hadn't even been there! I was sitting at home waiting for the man to come and mend my washing machine!

MAN. It's nice when you have a chance to get your own back, though. I rang up some place today and really gave some old cow what-for. Did the old heart good, I can tell you. Well, I'd stood in this shop waiting half-an-hour to be served!

WOMAN. Yes, I rang this firm up when I got to work and really let this fellow have it. Told him I'd ring their Chairman at home. That soon shut him up.

MAN. I said, "Am I by any chance entitled to some kind of cup or medal as a reward for long service?"

WOMAN. What I can't bear is when they try and fob you off by coming over all greasy and humble.

MAN. Oh, that sort! This woman was like that.

WOMAN. So was this man. Ugh! Some people!

MAN. Some right ones around, aren't there?

WOMAN. Nice to come in here and find there's still someone human left in the world.

HEAD TO HEAD

. . . gives me very great pleasure to be here—to see your beautiful and historic country for myself, and to bring greetings from my people across the sea to the people of Fandangia.

And here I must say what especial pleasure it gives me to be in Fandangia as the guest of President Goizi. (*Applause.*) In the hearts and in the affections of my countrymen, President Goizi will always hold a special place. We know how faithfully he has served Fandangia. We have watched him at the helm through times that have not always been easy, amidst the perilous shoals of our world today.

I may say that I had the privilege and good fortune to meet the previous President, President Fasces. It seems only yesterday that I was paying tribute to him at a not entirely dissimilar occasion. But it was in fact the day before yesterday, and since his tragic death early this morning President Goizi has shown himself in every way a worthy successor.

But we, in our country, have a special reason for the affection in which we hold President Goizi. For we know that the warm and friendly relations that exist between our two nations today are due in no small measure to his interest and to his unremitting efforts. It is perhaps not out of place to recall that President Goizi has visited us. He has seen us at work and play. He has tasted a sample of our national cooking (*Laughter.*)—and, I am assured pronounced it not greatly inferior to Fandangian cooking (*Laughter.*). He has watched our national game (*Laughter.*)—and, I believe, declared himself mystified by it (*Loud laughter.*). In short, we know that he has seen us at first hand, in times that have not always been easy, and observed how we have faced the perils that confront every nation in the world today. It is bonds like these that unite our two peoples (*Applause.*).

But we must not let our sense of history make us unaware of the changing world in which we live. We must not let our regard for tradition, and for the preservation of what is best in our way of life— important as these things are—blind us to the events which are taking place about us. And at this point it is perhaps not inappropriate that I should say how particularly pleased I am to find myself in Fandangia as the guest of President Bombardos (*Applause.*)

In terms of the time in which these things are measured, it might perhaps be said that President Bombardos has not been responsible for guiding Fandangia's destinies for very long. But already, since he took over the duties which were so unexpectedly thrust upon him after the sudden retirement for health reasons of his predecessor, President Goizi, this evening, he has proved himself to be a worthy successor.

He has brought Fandangia through times which for all of us have not been without their difficulties. It is perhaps scarcely an exaggeration to say that he has made this nation what it is at the moment. And in the hearts and minds of my countrymen, President Bombardos will always be assured of a special place. Already we have come to learn that in President Bombardos we have a true friend. I believe that it is not entirely inappropriate to recollect that he has spent some time among our people. One of his

special concerns was to study our police forces—
which he was kind enough to say were "wonderful"
(*Laughter.*). I believe he also had a taste of our
weather (*Laughter.*), though there is no record of his
saying the same thing about that. (*Loud laughter.*)

In other words, President Bombardos has seen us
as we are, looked at the best and worst in our nation,
and, as we like to think, come to understand us. For
us, President Bombardos *is* Fandangia (*Prolonged
applause.*).

But I should not like you to think that this close and
friendly interest in every latest development is not
fully reciprocated. I cannot therefore finish without
paying personal tribute to the President of the
Fandangian Republic, President Goizi, who, with the
exception of a brief interregnum very recently, has
guided your destinies for so long . . .

GLYCERINE

HUSBAND. (*Enters.*) I've put the leftovers on the side. I don't know what you want to do with them ... I said, I've put the leftovers on the side.

WIFE. (*Looks up for an instant from the television screen.*) On the side. Right.

HUSBAND. (*Sits down.*) What's this then? What have you got yourself?

WIFE. (*Absorbed.*) I don't know. Some historical thing.

HUSBAND. What's it about?

WIFE. (*Sighing.*) He's in love with her, only she doesn't ... Tch ...

HUSBAND. Only she doesn't what?

WIFE. I don't know ... She's ... It's all in days gone by ...

HUSBAND. Who's *that?*

WIFE. I think he just ... lives there.

HUSBAND. Lives where?

WIFE. There.

HUSBAND. (*Impatiently.*) Where's the paper? I can't stand not knowing what I'm looking at.

WIFE. Well, he's the one we saw in that other thing. The thing about the man who was going to ... I don't know ... blow something up, wasn't he? Only they found out about it somehow, and ... I don't know ... It all took place abroad somewhere.

HUSBAND. '9.20 – Party Political Broadcast.'

WIFE. That's yesterday's.

HUSBAND. Why have we *never* got today's paper? What do you do with it? You know I hate sitting here not knowing what I'm looking at.

WIFE. Anyway, she's the one who's married to that man.

HUSBAND. Married to that man? What man? Which man?

WIFE. That man in that thing we saw about ... whatever it was ...

HUSBAND. Oh, blimey!

WIFE. They can't have children. I saw it in the paper. They've adopted two little boys ... They say she's got a lovely home ... four-poster bed ... antique commodes ... I don't know ...

HUSBAND. *Now* what's happening? She's on a ship now! A moment ago she was in prison! What's going on?

WIFE. She's on her way to find ... the other one.

HUSBAND. What other one?

WIFE. The one that's always eating toffees.

HUSBAND. Toffees? Toffees hadn't been invented then!

WIFE. In that commercial.

HUSBAND. You sit in front of that set in a trance. Do you know that? You haven't the slightest idea what's happening in front of your eyes ...

(*SHE smiles.*)

HUSBAND. What was that? I missed that. What did he say?

WIFE. (*Sighs.*) I don't know. Something about I prithee something.

HUSBAND. You don't even know what they're saying!

WIFE. I can't *hear* what they're saying with you going jabber jabber all the time, who's this, who's that?

HUSBAND. If you don't know what he said, what are you sniggering at it for? Honestly, you let that television set turn you into a moron. I mean, I'm not anti-television. Far from it. Television can educate and stimulate the mind—if you watch it *actively*. If you *discuss* what you're watching and really try to ... He'll get his bloody head chopped off if he leaves it there...

WIFE. Tch.

HUSBAND. I told you ... I mean, if you took an interest in how it's done. For instance, *that*. Do you know how they do her tears? You don't think she can just cry to order?

(*SHE discreetly sheds a few tears herself.*)

HUSBAND. That's glycerine. Little drops of glycerine running down her face. Exactly the same as that stuff in the bathroom cabinet that you put on your hands in winter. Combined with nitrogen it forms nitro-glycerine, the well-known explosive. I mean, if you had a critical attitude. If you just asked yourself whether you're really enjoying it. Are you enjoying *this*?

WIFE. (*Sniffling.*) I don't know. I'm just watching it, that's all.

HUSBAND. Well, *think*, then! Make an effort for once! Use your brain! That's what God gave it to you for ...!

(*The words trail away. HE gazes at the screen, hypnotized. So does his wife, her tears forgotten. There is a long silence.*)

WIFE. Tch.
HUSBAND. Tch.

(*Then suddenly THEY both relax, and move uncomfortably about in their chairs.*)

HUSBAND. *That's* what you should be asking yourself—why they put all this sex in that no one wants to watch.

A PLEASURE SHARED

Do you spit? No? You don't mind if I do, though ...?

Khhghm ... Hold on—can you see a spittoon on the table anywhere...? Never mind. Sit down, sit down! I can use my empty soup bowl. Khhghm – *thpp!*

My God, that's better. No, I've been sitting here all the way through the first course just dying for one. Iron self-control, but I do think it's rather bad manners to spit while one's eating. I mean at a dinner party like this. Your mouth full of the hostess's soup, and suddenly ... kkhghm – *thpp!*

You *have* finished yourself, haven't you? You haven't! I'm so sorry ...! Oh, you don't want the rest.

Very nice of you not to ... khhghm – *thpp!* ... not to mind. One has to be so careful these days not to offend people's prejudices. I always ask first, of course. People never raise any objection, in my experience. In fact they usually never say anything at all. They generally do what you did—smile rather charmingly and kind of wave their hand about. Quite surprised even to be asked, I think, most of them.

Khhghm ... Where's the soup bowl gone ...? No, no—sit down! Don't keep jumping up! I'll use yours! You did say you'd finished ...? *Thpp!*

I'm glad you're not one of these hysterical people who try to stop other people enjoying themselves. It's so one-sided. I don't try to stop anyone *not* spitting over me! In fact this is something I feel rather strongly about. People used to spit all the time in the good old days, and no one so much as raised an eyebrow. Spittoons everywhere you went—sawdust on the floor. It was only about fifty years ago, you know, that all this anti-spitting nonsense started. Suddenly everyone went mad. Notices up in the buses—'No Spitting. Penalty £5.' And before we knew what had happened we'd lost another of our ancient liberties.

So, quite honestly, I ... Khhghm ... Oh, they've taken the soup bowls away ... No, no, stay right where you are! *Thpp!* ... Keeps the moth out of the tablecloth ... Yes, I spit very largely as a matter of principle.

And I hawk. As you can hear. Khhghm ...! In fact I hawk *deeply*, also as a matter of principle. *Khhhhhghhhhm* ...! Because I believe that if you're going to spit you might as well get the full benefit of it, and shift the entire contents of your lungs out into the atmosphere. Why keep all that stuff festering inside you, when you could so easily ... Khhghm – *thpp!* ... spread it around a bit ...?

Didn't spit in your face then, did I? Hold on—I think I did! I'm so sorry. I'll just give it a wipe with the corner of the tablecloth ...Come back, come back! The tablecloth's perfectly ... no, sorry, hold on, I'll try another bit ... There we are. It's very nice of you to go on smiling about it, but I know even the most broad-minded non-spitters sometimes feel a little sensitive about getting a faceful of the stuff.

Anyway point taken! I'll be very careful henceforth to turn my head aside, look, and ... Khhghm—*thpp!* ... spit in your lovely hair, or down your very charming dress.

Why don't I sit a little closer? There ... It's the alluring way you're ... khhghm – *thpp!* ... wriggling around! I beg your pardon ...? It tickles? What tickles?

You mean it ran down inside your dress? It gets everywhere, doesn't it! Anyway, don't worry! Just hang your underwear up in some airy place when you get home tonight, and it'll be dry in no time.

Look, you wouldn't mind, would you, if ... No, come here! Don't lean away! I'm trying to whisper a few private words in your ear. You wouldn't mind, would you, if I gave you a ring some time? I thought perhaps you might like to come round one evening. I could give you a quiet spot of ... Khhghm – *thpp!* Or we might go out and do something a little more exciting. I don't know. Maybe – Khhghhkhkhkhm – *thppshmk!*

You keep shaking your head. Did you get some in your ear? Don't worry—it's not as if you were inhaling it ... What? Oh, you're saying no? I see. I see. You're not somehow offended because you got a tiny bit in your eye ...? I though so! I *thought* that smile of yours was beginning to get a little fixed. My God! I did *ask*, if you remember. I did ask if you minded!

So you're one of these anti-spitting fanatics, are you? I'm not allowed to spit—is that what you're telling me?—but it's perfectly all right for you to go round leaning away from people, and grinning that ghastly glassy grin at them.

God, the *intolerance* of your lot! It makes me want to ... Well, I'll tell you what it makes me want to do. It makes me want to *khhhhhhghhhhhm* – Oh, and here's the next course. I'll put that one back for later.

SONS AND CUSTOMERS

MOTHER. Chocolates! Well, that *is* kind of you, Ralph. What with flowers from you, John, and bath salts from you, Howard, and you all three driving down to see me like this, I *am* having a lovely birthday! You shouldn't have bothered, you know, I'm sure you've all got much more important things to think about.

RALPH. That's all right, Mother—you only get a birthday once a year, you know. Incidentally, John, do you know where I bought these chocolates? Stanmores in Creese End Broadway.

JOHN. I thought you always bought your sweets and cigarettes in that branch of Goodmans opposite Wemblemore tube station?

RALPH. I used to. But I changed to Stanmores.

HOWARD. Well, you surprise me, Ralph. I thought you swore by Goodmans.

RALPH. I did. But do you know, I think you get better service at Stanmores. I really do.

JOHN. That's you all over, Ralph—chopping and changing until you find something that really suits you.

MOTHER. Ralph always was the adventurous one.

JOHN. I admire you for it, Ralph. But I couldn't do it myself. I mean, those flowers—I bought them at Gossards in Boylesden High Street. Now I've been buying flowers at Gossards for 15 years or more.

RALPH. I know you have, John, I know you have.

JOHN. They know me there. They know my name, they know my children's names, they know the sort of flowers I like. Well, they *know* me.

HOWARD. There is such a thing as loyalty, isn't there, after all? Look at me, I've been taking my car into the Upsome branch of Qualitimotors for 10 years now. They know me. They know the car.

JOHN. You know they care about you. You know you're someone to them.

HOWARD. I always feel they're genuinely pleased to see me in Qualitimotors. And not just me. They're pleased to see the car.

JOHN. I mean, today for instance. I was going to buy the carnations. But the manager said to me, he said: "Frankly, Mr. Tooting, they're not worth it." I mean, he was quite frank with me. "They're not worth the money, Mr. Tooting," he said. "I know you, Mr. Tooting, and if I were you I'd pay just that little bit more and have the chrysanths."

RALPH. Oh, I agree. I agree.

JOHN. They know I won't stand any nonsense.

MOTHER. When it comes to nonsense, a very strange thing happened to me once in a shop in Singapore.

JOHN. Just you sit back and enjoy yourself, Mother. It's your birthday, remember.

RALPH. No, as I was saying, John, I agree with you. Take me now. I get my wines and spirits from a little man in Dorris Hill.

HOWARD. "Simon the Cellarer" in Manor Park Road, isn't it?

RALPH. That's right. Run by a chap called Nuthall. Been dealing with him for donkey's years now, and when it comes to wines, well, I trust his judgment. "You know, Mr. Tooting," he said to me once, "I never need to ask you—I know it's not the cheap stuff you'll be wanting." Proper character, old Nuthall. And if he gets the orders mixed up he'll always take it back without any argument.

HOWARD. It's the same with me at Qualitimotors. I always deal with the foreman, of course.

JOHN. Yes, it's the manager who always serves me at Gossards.

HOWARD. "Hello, Mr. Tooting," he says when I go in. "The old clutch playing up again?" And ready to oblige! Well, I've taken the same repair on the clutch back six times to get it right without anyone saying a word.

JOHN. Mark you, you pay for it.

RALPH. Oh, of course you do. But then you and I expect to pay a bit over the odds. Some people are happy to buy stuff on the cheap, and good luck to them. But you and I have been brought up differently.

HOWARD. Though it's not just a matter of money, of course. I mean, you go into Qualitimotors in a Jag, flashing a roll of notes, and I don't suppose they'd reckon much to you. But you go in and say I sent you and I think you can be pretty sure they'll look after you all right.

RALPH. If it comes to that, I think you'll find my name's a pretty good passport anywhere along Creese End or Dorris Hill.

HOWARD. Well, in Higgins and Dickens you've only to mention my name and they'll give you the freedom of the shop.

JOHN. I'm not exaggerating, Howard, but if I so much as raised an eyebrow in Higgins and Dickens they'd get down on their hands and knees and clean my boots.

RALPH. Without a word of a lie, John, I could walk down Creese End Broadway tomorrow and have my boots *licked* clean by the manager of every quality shop in turn.

JOHN. Mark you, I think we've a right to it. I think I can say in all honesty I'm a pretty good customer of Higgins and Dickens.

HOWARD. Yes, we're all pretty good customers.

RALPH. Well, we all sincerely *try* to be good customers. You can't do more than that, can you?

MOTHER. Just so long as you try to be good, dear, God will understand.

HEAVEN

GEOFFREY. Another beautiful day. Heaven really looks at its best on a day like this.

JEAN. Heaven always looks at its best.

GEOFFREY. Yes, doesn't it. Every time I have to come up here to the Acts of God Directorate I'm rather ... I don't know ... *moved.* Those golden streets. That amethyst archway in front of the Recording Angel's office. I'm ... oddly attached to this place, you know, Jean.

JEAN. Aren't we all?

GEOFFREY. You're very lucky here in Small Catastrophes. Having this view over the Major Disasters building. All these sapphires and chalcedonies and sardonyxes flashing in the sun. Every time I come up here for a meeting and see this view I'm oddly ... I don't know ...

JEAN. Moved.

GEOFFREY. Yes. Aren't you?

JEAN. Of course.

GEOFFREY. We're all very lucky, really. I can't help feeling sometimes that we're all rather ... well ...

JEAN. Privileged to be here. Yes. All right, Geoffrey, what have I done wrong this time?

GEOFFREY. (*Laughs.*) 'Done wrong!' Good. Yes. Very witty.

JEAN. Well, then, what have I done less right than I should have?

GEOFFREY. Jean, this chap you're going to kill in Norfolk.

JEAN. You don't want me to kill him?

GEOFFREY. Of course I want you to kill him. But you've got him down to be killed by an avalanche. Dear Jean, if you so wish, *of course*. But do you realize the cost of producing an avalanche in Norfolk? In terms of ecological damage and disruption to life? We'd have to throw up a complete range of mountains first!

JEAN. Geoffrey, we must have this out once and for all. Whatever way I put forward to kill people it doesn't meet with your approval! I say, we'll drop a slate on his head. You immediately come running up here and say, do I appreciate just how much wind we have to let loose to dislodge a slate? Geoffrey, I don't *care* how much wind we have to let loose, or how many mountains we have to push up! You see? It doesn't interest me.

GEOFFREY. Jean—dear Jean—my job, my humble task in this organization, is to protect the innocent ...

JEAN. And my job's to kill them! There's a definite policy clash here. Every method I come up with—tidal waves, giant hailstones, earth tremors—you try to block it!

GEOFFREY. Jean, Jean, Jean! I'm not blocking anything! All I'm saying is, does it have to be this particular man in Norfolk? Couldn't you bring the avalanche down on someone who lives at the foot of a mountain already?

JEAN. But that would be *banal!* The whole *point* of the operation is to enrich the texture of life! To engender a certain sense of wonder at the possibilities of the world! To keep alive a sense of awe! You must expect to make a few sacrifices for that.

GEOFFREY. Well, Jean, I think there's a lot to be said for the good, old-fashioned, well-tried ...

JEAN. Flash of lightning.

GEOFFREY. Particularly in Norfolk.

JEAN. Oh, Geoffrey! I sometimes wonder if you really love me.

GEOFFREY. Of course I love you.

JEAN. As much as I love you?

GEOFFREY. As much as we all of us here love each other.

AN OCCASION OF THIS NATURE

There always, I'm afraid, comes the dread moment at an occasion of this nature when someone gets up on his or her hind legs and makes a speech. That moment has now come! I know that the last thing anyone here wants to do is to listen to a speech, just when everyone was enjoying themselves, and the last thing *I* want to do is to make a speech, believe me, but I do think that we cannot let an occasion of this nature go by without stopping for just a moment to say a few words about how worthwhile and enjoyable an occasion of this nature is. We all take things for granted only too easily—I know I do—and I think if no one took the trouble to just stand up for a moment and put it into words, we might just possibly all sit here and not realize quite what a worthwhile and enjoyable time we were in fact having.

It cannot, I think, be said too often that an occasion of this nature doesn't just happen of its own accord. Let's all have a good time and enjoy ourselves, by all means. But let's try to bear in mind as we do so all the hard work and long hours and personal sacrifice that have gone into it. And I must just say here, before I forget, that Mr. Pettigrew tells me there are still a great many tickets unsold for the Grand Lucky Draw. So can we all put our backs into it and make one last effort? There are some splendid prizes to be won, and anyway the prizes are not what counts. Oh yes, and would people *please* not put unwanted sandwiches or other matter into the heating vents? I know how easy it is for little fingers to do—perhaps even for fingers that *aren't* quite so little!—but getting small pieces of decaying fishpaste out again with knitting needles and surgical forceps, as we had to do last year, does waste a lot of the limited time available for committee meetings.

I should just like to say a word of thanks to the many people involved in making today a success, I'm sure that having their name mentioned was the last thing they had in mind in the first place, and they'll probably never forgive me, but I hope they'll forgive me if there are any names I forget to mention.

First and foremost, of course, our heartiest thanks are due once again to Mrs. Paramount. I'm sure I don't have to tell you that without Mrs. Paramount an occasion of this nature simply could not take place. This is, in a very special sense, her baby—and has been so ever since the late Lord Combermere on his death bed first planted the seed.

Our thanks are also due, in no less measure, to Mr. Huddle for his unfailing cheerfulness, and his apparent readiness in emergencies to dash almost anywhere in the middle of the night, clad in old army boots and Manchester United scarf. And I should like to say a special word of thanks to Mr. Hapforth, who came along here tonight against doctor's orders, and in spite of being in considerable pain. I think perhaps we might remember that when we see him struggling to entertain us all once again.

Last but not least I should like to thank all of you for coming along here today, and working so hard to enjoy the entertainment that all these good people have worked so hard to provide. It's particularly gratifying to see so many young faces. We often think of young people today as simply out for a good time.

Well, that certainly can't be said of these young people. It's no less gratifying to see all the people here who aren't quite so young. I know how easy it is to think, "Oh let someone else go out this time and get themselves entertained." I must say, it's remarkable how an occasion of this nature seems to bring out the best in people. Everyone rallies round, and cheerfully tries to make the best of it. It's like the War all over again! I'd just like to say this: it's people like you who make an occasion of this nature the sort of occasion that it is. I'm sure you'll be pleased to hear that as a result of everyone's efforts today and over the past year we have raised the very gratifying total of £23.17.

Well you don't want to sit here listening to me talk, and I certainly don't want to stand here talking, so I'm going to sit down and let Mr. Dauntwater stand up and speak. Mr. Dauntwater, I should explain, has kindly agreed at very short notice to make the speech thanking me for my speech. So, in the sudden but unavoidable absence of Mrs. Hummer with gastric trouble, and to save time later on, I should just like if I might to thank Mr. Dauntwater for his speech in advance. And thank you all for listening to me. And remember! Not in the heating vents!

THE MESSENGER'S ASSISTANT

Enter MEANDER, an ill-fated king.

MEANDER
Oh, who would choose my hapless destiny?
To be a king, with naught to do but wait
For messengers from other parts of Greece
With mournful news of yet some new disaster;
Of madness in Thebes, of rape in Thessaly;
Of slow revenge and murder everywhere;
Of oracles predicting worse to come.
The signs portend another messenger
Today. What tragic tale will he unfold?
What solemn threnody of unseen woe?
But look! He is approaching even now!
And from his face I fear his news will prove
More pain to bear than all the rest. Yet stay!
Someone comes with him. A woman. What is this?

Enter a MESSENGER and his WIFE.

MESSENGER
O most unhappy king!

WIFE
It's terrible!

MESSENGER
O ruler cursed by fate!

WIFE
            It's tragic, really.
I told them it would happen! I saw it coming!
Now put that sword away, I said, before
Some accident occurs. But would they listen?

MESSENGER
I am, O King, a messenger from Thrace ...

WIFE
And I'm his wife. I help him with his work.
I go on all his business trips—I have to!
He's hopeless if you leave him to himself!
He always gets the story wrong! Leaves out
The best bits—gets the point all back to front!
A messenger? I send him out to buy
A leg of lamb, and back he comes with goat!

MESSENGER
What is man's life? What is man's destiny?

WIFE
Get on with it! He doesn't want to stand
And wait all day while you philosophise!

MESSENGER
Know, then, ill-omen'd king, there stands in Thrace
A grove of sacred alders by a brook,
Where innocent maids delight to weave their
   garlands...

WIFE
We had a picnic there the other week!
We always like to get out when it's fine.
We took some sandwiches—I made a cake.

Just us. It was nice. Of course, we never *dreamed!*

MESSENGER
All unsuspecting to this guileless grove
Came Ichtheumon, the son of Polyphonius ...

WIFE
Blood everywhere! You wouldn't believe the mess!

MEANDER
Ichtheumon! My cousin once removed? Is dead?
Thus has the ancient prophecy been fulfilled!

MESSENGER
No, no!

WIFE
No, no!

MESSENGER
Not Ichtheumon.

WIFE
The other one!

MESSENGER
Diameter.

WIFE
Diameter!

MEANDER
The son
Of Radius? Can it be?

MESSENGER
It fell out thus:
Unto the rustling alders in the grove
Came Ichtheumon, and Agone, his sister ...

WIFE
Wearing a chlamys that her mother made
From a tablecloth her aunt brought back from Persia.

MESSENGER
Now in this grove there sat a gnarled old man,
And slowly, wondering much, they recognised
In him Phlogiston, who was driven forth
From Argos by a jealous royal house ...

WIFE
I'd like to hang them all, I really would.

MESSENGER
... for slaying Chloros, son of Aspidistra,
In vengeance for the death of Rhododendron.

WIFE
I hate to interrupt. I know how cross
You get. But time and time again I've told you—
Chloros wasn't Aspidistra's son,
But Oxygenia's child by her first husband!
She later married Neon. In white. Some people!

MEANDER
This is indeed a painful tale to bear.

MESSENGER
In any case, Phlogiston now was here,
Fleeing the wrath of Archipelagos ...

WIFE

No, dear! Not Archipelagos at all!
It was Parenthesis, for heaven's sake!
You're muddling it with the job you had last week
Of telling Oxymoron that his children
Had been expelled from school for matricide!

MESSENGER

Fleeing the wrath of Archipelagos!

WIFE

This is embarrassing! Quite how you got
A job as messenger I can't imagine.

MESSENGER

The wrath belonged to Archipelagos!
Another messenger told me this morning!

WIFE

But he was probably just as bad as you!
I don't suppose he had his wife with him
To put him right on just this kind of detail!

MESSENGER

Excuse me.

(*HE takes his Wife off.*)

MEANDER

Why do they always do it out of sight?

(*A SCREAM off.*)

MEANDER
We'll have a memorandum now on this!

MESSENGER
(*Enter, alone.*)

At last! A bloody deed I can recount
Without the slightest fear of interruption!

The End

Value for Money, Blots, Who Do You Think You Are?, Heaven, Confession, The Messenger's Assistant, Listen to This, and *Glycerine* were first seen in Eleanor Bron's television series, *Beyond a Joke,* in 1972.

An Occasion of this Nature was first performed by Eleanor Bron at an Amnesty evening (*The Secret Policeman's Ball?*) in 1979.

A Bit of Peace and Quiet and *Never Mind the Weather* have not been performed or published.

Head to Head first appeared in the *Guardian,* and is reproduced here by permission of the Editor. It was first published in book form in *The Book of Fub* (Collins, 1963). *A Pleasure Shared* first appeared in *The Independent.* The remaining pieces first appeared in *The Observer,* and appear here by permission of the Editor. They were first published in book form in *On The Outskirts* (Collins, 1964).

Other Publications for Your Interest

MOVIE OF THE MONTH
(COMEDY)
By DANIEL MELTZER

2 men—Interior

This new comedy by the author of the ever-popular *The Square Root of Love* is an amusing satire of commercial television. B.S., a TV programming executive, is anxious to bolster his network's ratings, which have been sagging of late due to programming disasters such as a documentary called "The Ugly Truth" (says B.S.: "What the hell is The Ugly Truth, and how the hell did it get into our Prime Time?") His eagerbeaver assistant, appropriately named Broun, has found a script which he is sure can be made into a hit "Movie of the Month". It's about this Danish prince, see, who comes home from college to find that his uncle has murdered his father and married his mother . . . Well, naturally, B.S. has his own ideas about how to fix such a totally unbelievable plot . . .   (#17621)

SUNDANCE
(ALL GROUPS—COMEDY)
By MEIR Z. RIBALOW

5 men—Simple interior

This new comedy from the author of *Shrunken Heads* is set in a sort of metaphysical wild west saloon. The characters include Hickock, Jesse, the Kid, and the inevitable Barkeep. Hickock kills to uphold the law. Jesse kills for pleasure. The Kid kills to bring down The Establishment. What if, wonders the Barkeep, they met up with the Ultimate Killer—who kills for no reason, who kills simply because that's what he does? Enter Sundance. He does not kill to uphold the law, for pleasure, or to make a political statement, or because he had a deprived childhood. And he proceeds to kill everyone, exiting at the end with his sixguns blazing! "Witty, strong, precise, unusually well-written."—The Guardian. "A brilliant piece."—Dublin Evening Press. This co-winner of the 1981 Annual NYC Metropolitan Short Play Festival has been a success in 6 countries!   (#3113)

Other Publications for Your Interest

ADVICE TO THE PLAYERS
(DRAMA)

By BRUCE BONAFEDE

5 men, 1 woman (interracial)—Interior

Seldom has a one-act play created such a sensation as did *Advice to the Players* at Actors Theatre of Louisville's famed Humana Festival of New American Plays. Mr. Bonafede has crafted an ingenious play about two Black South African actors, here in America to perform their internationally-acclaimed production of *Waiting for Godot*. The victims of persecution in their own country, here in the U.S. they become the victims of a different kind of persecution. The anti-apartheid movement wants a strong political gesture—they want the performance cancelled. And, they are willing to go to any lengths to achieve this aim—including threatening the families of the actors back home. Cleverly, Mr. Bonafede juxtaposes the predicament of Didi and Gogo in *Waiting for Godot* with the predicament of the two actors. Both, in an odd, ironic way, are Theatre of the Absurd. "A short play blazing with emotional force and moral complexities . . . taut, searing inquiry into the inequities frequently perpetrated in the name of political justice . . . a stunning moment of theatrical truth."—Louisville Courier-Journal.   (#3027)

APPROACHING LAVENDAR
(COMIC DRAMA)

By JULIE BECKETT CRUTCHER

3 women—Interior

While their father is marrying his fourth wife sardonic, controlled Jenny and her slightly neurotic housewife-sister Abigail wait in a church vestibule. There they encounter Wren, the spacey ingenue who is about to become their step-sister. The mood of polite tolerance degenerates with comic results as inherent tensions mount and the womens' conflicted feelings about their parents' remarriage surface. The contingent self-discovery results in new understanding and forgiveness, and ultimately reveals the significance of sisterhood. Highly-praised in its debut at the famed Actors Theatre of Louisville, the play was singled out by the Louisville press for its "precise and disquieting vision" as well as its sharp humor, as it "held a capacity audience rapt."   (#3649)

A TANTALIZING
(DRAMA)

By WILLIAM MASTROSIMONE

1 man, 1 woman—Interior

Originally produced by the amazing Actors Theatre of Louisville, this is a new one-act drama by the author of *The Woolgatherer* and *Extremities*. *A Tantalizing* is about the attempts by a young woman to "save" a street bum, a tattered and crazy old man whom she has dragged in off the street. Like Rose in *Extremities* she, too, has secrets in her closet. What these secrets are is the intriguing mystery in the plot of the play, as we gradually realize why the woman has taken such an interest in the bum.   (#22021)

Other Publications for Your Interest

PASTORAL
(COMEDY)

By PETER MALONEY

1 man, 1 woman—Exterior

Daniel Stern ("Blue Thunder", "Breaking Away") and Kristin Griffith ("The Europeans", "Interiors") starred originally at NYC's famed Ensemble Studio Theatre in the preceptive comedy about a city couple temporarily tending a farm. He hates the bucolic life and is terrified, for instance, by such horrors as a crowing rooster; whereas she is at one with the land *and* the rooster. "An endearing picture of young love at a comic crossroads."—N.Y. Times. "Sharp, satiric humor."—New Yorker. "An audience pleaser."—Village Voice. Published with *Last Chance Texaco*. (#17995)

LAST CHANCE TEXACO
(DRAMA)

By PETER MALONEY

3 women—Interior

Originally staged to great acclaim at NYC's famed Ensemble Studio Theatre, this is a haunting, lyrical play set in the American Garage, a Texaco station in a small Texas town run by a mother and her daughter. Late one night, while driving through, a city woman named Ruth has a flat tire, an occurrence which causes her own unusual life to intersect with Verna and Cissy, as they fix her tire in the American Garage. This play is an excellent source of monologue and scene material. It is also a gripping piece of theatre. Published with *Pastoral*. (#13887)

BUSINESSMAN'S LUNCH
(COMEDY)

By MICHAEL QUINN

4 men, 1 woman—Interior

Originally produced by the famed Actors Theatre of Louisville, this marked the debut of a wonderful new comic playwriting voice. We are in one of those quiche-and-salad restaurants, where three high-powered young executives of a nearby candy company are having lunch as they discuss company politics and various marketing and advertising strategies. They particularly enjoy making fun of one of their fellows who is not present, whom they consider a hopeless nerd—until, that is, they learn that he is engaged to marry the boss's daughter. "Cleverly skewers corporate stereotypes."—NY Times. (#4712)

Other Publications for Your Interest

NOISES OFF
(LITTLE THEATRE—FARCE)

By MICHAEL FRAYN

5 men, 4 women—2 Interiors

This wonderful Broadway smash hit is "a farce about farce, taking the clichés of the genre and shaking them inventively through a series of kaleidoscopic patterns. Never missing a trick, it has as its first act a pastiche of traditional farce; as its second, a contemporary variant on the formula; as its third, an elaborate undermining of it. The play opens with a touring company dress-rehearsing 'Nothing On', a conventional farce. Mixing mockery and homage, Frayn heaps into this play-within-a-play a hilarious melee of stock characters and situations. Caricatures—cheery char, outraged wife and squeaky blonde—stampede in and out of doors. Voices rise and trousers fall . . . a farce that makes you think as well as laugh."—London Times Literary Supplement. ". . . as side-splitting a farce as I have seen. Ever? *Ever.*"—John Simon, NY Magazine. "The term 'hilarious' must have been coined in the expectation that something on the order of this farce-within-a-farce would eventually come along to justify it."—N.Y. Daily News. "Pure fun."—N.Y. Post. "A joyous and loving reminder that the theatre really does go on, even when the show falls apart."—N.Y. Times.   (#16052)

THE REAL THING
(ADVANCED GROUPS—COMEDY)

By TOM STOPPARD

4 men, 3 women—Various settings

The effervescent Mr. Stoppard has never been more intellectually—and *emotionally*—engaging than in this "backstage" comedy about a famous playwright named Henry Boot whose second wife, played on Broadway to great acclaim by Glenn Close (who won the Tony Award), is trying to merge "worthy causes" (generally a euphemism for left-wing politics) with her art as an actress. She has met a "political prisoner" named Brodie who has been jailed for radical thuggery, and who has written an inept play about how property is theft, about how the State stifles the Rights of The Individual, etc., etc., etc. Henry's wife wants him to make the play work theatrically, which he does after much soul-searching. Eventually, though, he is able to convince his wife that Brodie is emphatically *not* a victim of political repression. He is, in fact, a *thug*. Famed British actor Jeremy Irons triumphed in the Broadway production (Tony Award), which was directed to perfection by none other than Mike Nichols (Tony Award). "So densely and entertainingly packed with wit, ideas and feelings that one visit just won't do . . . Tom Stoppard's most moving play and the most bracing play anyone has written about love and marriage in years."—N.Y. Times. "Shimmering, dazzling theatre, a play of uncommon wit and intelligence which not only thoroughly delights but challenges and illuminates our lives."—WCBS-TV. 1984 Tony Award-Best Play.   (#941)

Other Publications for Your Interest

THE SQUARE ROOT OF LOVE
(ALL GROUPS—FOUR COMEDIES)
By DANIEL MELTZER

1 man, 1 woman—4 Simple Interiors

This full-length evening portrays four preludes to love—from youth to old age, from inno-cence to maturity. Best when played by a single actor and actress. **The Square Root of Love.** Two genius-level college students discover that Man (or Woman) does not live by intellectual pursuits alone . . . **A Good Time for a Change.** Our couple are now a suc-cessful executive and her handsome young male secretary. He has decided it's time for a change, and so has she . . . **The Battling Brinkmires.** George and Marsha Brinkmire, a middle-aged couple, have come to Haiti to get a "quickie" divorce. This one has a surprise ending . . . **Waiting For To Go.** We are on a jet waiting to take off for Florida. He's a re-tired plumbing contractor who thinks his life is over—she's a recent widow returning to her home in Hallandale. The play, and the evening, ends with a beginning . . . A success at off-off Broadway's Hunter Playwrights. Requires only minimal settings.   (#21314)

SNOW LEOPARDS
(LITTLE THEATRE—COMIC DRAMA)
By MARTIN JONES

2 women—Exterior

This haunting little gem of a play was a recent crowd-pleaser Off Off Broadway in New York City, produced by the fine StageArts Theatre Co. Set in Lincoln Park Zoo in Chicago in front of the snow leopards' pen, the play tells the story of two sisters from rural West Virginia. When we first meet Sally, she has run away from home to find her big sister Claire June, whose life Up North she has imagined to be filled with all the promise and hopes so lacking Down Home. Turns out, life in the Big City ain't all Sally and C.J. thought it would be: but Sally is going to stay anyway, and try to make her way. "Affecting and carefully crafted . . . a moving piece of work."—New York City Tribune. *Actresses take note*: this play is a treasure trove of scene and monologue material. *Producers take note*: the play may be staged simply and inexpensively.   (#21245)